Ordinary

(First editi...
English language ...ion.

Poetry Series. Volume 1

A Collection of Poems & Explanatory Prose

by
Mark T. Watson

With a Fore-Word from "Jalal" of "The Last Poets".

Ordinary Guy

By
Mark T. Watson.

**Editorial consultant,
Bill Harpe MA (Cantab.) Guardian columnist.**

Published by Fore-Word™ Press Ltd.
Poetry Series. Volume 1.

First edition (English language version).
First published in the United Kingdom 2004 by
Fore-Word™ Press Ltd.
Registered office: 88 Rodney Street, Liverpool. L1 9AR. England. UK.
Tel/Fax: +44 (0)151 726 0304
Email:info@fore-word.com Website: http://www.fore-word.com

© Abdul Malik Al Nasir 2004
All rights reserved. No part of this book may be reproduced or adapted
in any form known or to become know, now or at any time in the future,
in any place by mechanical, electronic or other means of copying,
printing, storage, retrieval, transmission, performance, broadcast,
(whether terrestrial or extra terrestrial i.e. satellite) dramatic, literary,
theatrical or musical production of any sort whatsoever without the
prior written permission of Fore-Word™ Press Ltd. or their duly authorised agents and subject to the terms thereof or those terms agreed
with duly authorised reprographic, performing or other relevant rights
organisations or as expressly permitted by law.

The moral rights of the author Mark T. Watson have been asserted.
Cover illustration concept by Sarah McKenzie.
All pictures © Abdul Malik Al Nasir 2004 except photo (Hajj-Jalal/Malik)
courtesy of Yousuf Linjawi; student at Al Andalus School KSA,
by kind permission. http://www.alandalus-school.edu
"Malik's Mode" © Abdul Malik Al Nasir 2004. Written by Jalal Nuriddin
of "The Last Poets". Email Jalal via: http://www.grandfatherofrap.com

British Library Cataloguing in Publication Data.
A catalogue record for this book is available from the British Library.

ISBN 0-9548867-0-4 (Pbk)

Typesetting by Fore-Word™ Press Ltd.
Typeset in Arial 11pt.
Printed via Canongate Books, 14 High Street,
Edinburgh. EH1 1TE. Scotland. UK.
Tel:+44 (0)131 557 5111
Fax:+44 (0)131 557 5211
Email: info@canongate.co.uk
www.canongate.net

Distributed in the UK by
Central Books Ltd, 99 Wallis Road, London. E9 5LN. England. UK.
Tel:+44(0)845 458 9911 Fax:+44(0)845 458 9912
Email: info@centralbooks.com
www.centralbooks.com

All rights reserved.

Contents.

Contents.

List of illustrations.

Acknowledgements.

I would like to first thank my Lord, who guided me to the truth and gave me the inspiration and ability to write. Special thanks to my wife, Sarah McKenzie; who has stood by me throughout the whole painstaking process of preparing this compilation and has been a constant source of suggestions and support. My mum Sonia, my brother Reynold, sisters Michelle and Jackie and all the family's children. Thanks to Ramona Da Gama, Malcolm Cecil (Spice Inc.) Bill Harpe (Guardian columnist) and Aziz Al Mashal - may Allah reward you? Thanks to Haroob Mullick and his family, Muhammad Rashid, Eddie Amoo (The Real Thing), David, Dianne & Pete Wylie (WAH).

Big thanks to Gil Scott Heron's 'Amnesia Express'. Robbie Gordon 'the secretary of entertainment' - aka Muhammad Abdul Hadi, for years of encouragement, support and sheer brotherhood. Larry McDonald 'the rhythm master' for that old-school advice and guidance. Rod Youngs 'the master of disaster' (and his wife Nafisa). Kim Jordan, Ron Holloway, Steve Walker, Lyn Oakey, Dave McClean 'the sound man', Ed' Brady, Ibrahim Shakur 'Ibo', Kenny Powell, Vernon James, Leon Williams and the late Don McGriggs. Also Gil Scott Heron's Midnight Band', including; Glen 'Astro' Turner - aka Bilal Yusef, Bilal Sunni Ali, Tony Duncanson 'the timbale man', Barnett Williams 'the doc' and Brian Jackson - aka Hakim.

I cannot amply express my thanks to Jamie Byng, who inspired me to believe in my own ability to write this book and has provided expert and valuable advice in getting this book to publication. Also, all the wonderful staff at Canongate Books; Jenny Vass, Jules Thompson, Francis Bickmore et al, who have from time to time, assisted in various ways.

Also major thanks to Hugh Potter, Amanda Dunn, Mr. A.M. Azhar and James Rymer, for a job well done. Thanks to Dr. Martin Carey, Dean of Liverpool Hope University for believing in me and Prof. Ronaldo Munk. Also to Umar Hammerman, Khalid Al Jaddor, Bryan Parry, Mary and Brendan Manning who said, "The only freedom left in a democracy, is the freedom to write a book and publish it yourself." I'm eternally grateful to you all.

This book is dedicated to my
literary brothers and mentors

'Gil Scott Heron',
'Jalal M. Nuriddin' (The Last Poets)
& the late 'Suliman El Hadi'
(The Last Poets).

Special thanks to 'Michael Moore' for picking up
their political mantle and waking up the masses.

About the Author.

Born in the late sixties, Mark showed an early love of poetry, writing his first poem at the age of only 8 years, called "summertime". It was in celebration of getting off from school for the summer holidays.

His father was a merchant seaman, born in 1918 in a sugar cane plantation in Berbice, Demerara, British Guyana. His father's nickname was "Slow Train" as he'd walked 250 miles from London to Liverpool, seeking work in the 1950's after serving on the supply ships throughout World War II and in the battle of the Atlantic.

At the age of nine, Mark's world changed when his father had a stroke and became a quadriplegic. Mark was one of four siblings raised by his mother Sonia, who came to Liverpool from a little village in North Wales. A white woman raising four black kids in the 1970's was a clear social work case and inevitably, in 1975, Mark was taken into local authority care.

He emerged semi-literate from that era at the age of 18 years, with no formal qualifications and a bitter taste from the injustices he had both suffered and witnessed whilst in so-called "care". This was to spark a remarkable chain of events which caused him to challenge the system at all levels and compelled him to travel the globe in search of the truth.

The journey started with his meeting the infamous political poet and performer "Gil Scott Heron" who took Mark under his wing and schooled him in life. Mark has travelled on and off with Gil and his band from 1984 to the present day, touring the UK, Europe and the USA.

During these tours, Gil took it upon himself to mentor Mark and encouraged him to become productive, creative and educated. This mentoring, combined with close study of Gil Scott Heron's published work had a dramatic effect on Mark, fostering a real sense of social responsibility and a desire to both change himself and bring about positive changes in the world.

Mark left Gil for a few years and went away to sea. He used the long days to ponder nature and taught himself to read and write. He wrote to Gil regularly, sending copies of his poems for Gil's appraisal. This book largely derives from that period, inspired by Gil's knowledge and the value of his revolutionary poetic work, which not only inspired the black people of three generations in the States, but ricocheted throughout the world.

Mark returned from sea in 1990, armed with a command of language acquired from six hours per night of reading and writing on the ship. He took up a job in marketing and went to college to study business and finance. His high grades got him into University and despite the lack of formal education whilst in the so-called "care of the local authority", Mark graduated with honours in 1996, returning to read for an MSc. in 2000.

However, Mark's life was to take another dramatic turn before entering University. His unending quest for "the truth" which had guided him to Gil, was now leading him further back to those who had influenced his very mentor. In 1986, Mark had had a chance encounter with Jalal, leader of the 60's band "The Last Poets" after a gig in Liverpool. He told Jalal that he had worked with Gil, and Jalal said, "Stay with the righteous and you shall surely prosper."

Another chance meeting with Jalal happened in 1988 at the Town and Country venue in London where the Wailers (Bob Marley's band) were playing. Mark asked him, "How will I know who the righteous are?" And Jalal replied, "They won't be surrounded by the un-righteous." Mark had taken the advice of both Gil and Jalal and was now trying to retrace history in order to comprehend the injustices of racism, power and politics.

He was inspired by works like Gil's "The Revolution Will Not be Televised", "Cane", "B-Movie" and "We Beg Your Pardon America". Also, The Last Poets', "When the Revolution Comes", "Mean Machine", "Beyonder" and "The Hustlers Convention".

The poetic works of Langston Hughes, Paul Roberson and Maya Angelou and the literary works of Bell Hooks, Rosa Guy and Zora Neil Hurston to name but a few, gave him a sense of how he came to be a black man in England, via Afro-Caribbean slavery. However, it was to be the works of Alex Haley that would mark a turning point for Mark. After reading "Roots", his curiosity turned to rage and when followed up with the "autobiography of Malcolm X" suddenly it all made sense, racism, slavery - the lot.

Having read the autobiography of Malcolm X whilst on holiday in the Christmas of 1991, upon his return to the UK, he again met up with Jalal of The Last Poets, who after much questioning and providing comprehensible answers to all the outstanding mysteries of "life the universe and everything" (to coin a Douglas Adams phrase) Jalal introduced Mark to the faith of Islam.

Mark passed through University as a fledgling Muslim and wishing to put something back into those who had helped him in life, he introduced no fewer than 50 people to Islam in the first 10 years of his conversion. Three of these were members of Gil's band. Still feeling that he had unfinished business with the State who had so harmed him whilst in their care, Mark, - now named Malik Al Nasir - took legal action to sue the government for negligence. After much sacrifice and with the help of Allah, the government capitulated after 10 years of litigation and settled on the day of trial, before Judge Moreland at the High Court. He also received a public apology from the Lord Mayor of Liverpool.

This book is the first project that Malik has undertaken since then and is a tribute to Gil Scott Heron and Jalal for their selfless pursuit of truth and their unwavering stance for justice in the face of adversity but moreover for their compassion and spiritual guidance for someone like Mark, who was after all, just an *"Ordinary Guy".

---

*"Ordinary Guy" was a song title by Joe Bataan, an "Afro-Filipino".

Fore-Word
from "Jalal" of "The Last Poets".
"Malik's Mode".

A change from Mark to Malik was simply unique for a Liverpool youth. The truth in the face of stiff-upper-lip resistance. For this knowledge had been academically forbidden, obscured and hidden, at least up until that point in his existence.

His need to know, had begun to grow from the time that he was a child, to counter their racist obsession with perpetual oppression, that had him categorised as "wild".

From out of juvenile school, in Liverpool, he has fought his way to freedom. Just because of the colour of his skin, they locked him in, then held him down and beat him.

For this was commonplace, when it came to race and a tradition etched in stone. From a racist society, filled with a variety of traps to catch you alone.

Like myself, he was a victim of his past that was meant to last, until the end of time. That is unless you can free your mind and save your behind from a life of corruption and crime.

He sought me out, to dispel any doubt he had about the creator of the heavens and Earth. For he was searching for the One, whose will was being done and only he knew its worth.

For the "One" is sublime and the fashioner of time, who ordains what it is to be. All Mark had to do was seek, in order to become Malik, 'cause the truth will set you free.

He asked me a few questions and I answered with suggestions, that guided him on the way. For he was to be among those who believed, after having received the message without delay.

Since then he advanced after taking a stance, against those who had deceived him. And although he didn't know it, he too would become a poet, as well as an enlightened Muslim.

But that was Allah's plan, against which no one can stand, even if they insisted. Pharaoh was but one example and just a sample for all those who resisted.

Today brother Malik is a master at calling people to Allah and perpetuating the "Deen". And these poems in his book, are an early look, before he found Allah the 'One' the 'Supreme'.

Al Hemdu Lilahi Rabil Alamin -
(All praise is for Allah the Lord of all creation.)

"The Last Poets".

Poets.

1.
I sit and think of poets dead.
Of others living and what they've said.

I ponder curiously through their odes.
Their varied dialects confuse my thoughts.

My mind - the home of fantasies.
Imagination nurtured into verse
and words on paper to converse
with those who might just seek my view
and those who may remember you.

But view I must, also the verse
of those called "great" like Wordsworth
and Shakespeare, Shelley, Chaucer, Keats and
Robert Browning; school-work's sick!

So sick their talk of war and rape and gallant men
whose souls abase - the moral fibre of my life,
rammed down my throat by teachers' spite.

Yet school room text of men called "great"
in my existence can't relate.
Nor in my book they dare to lie
with sickened minds to fantasise.

And great by definition to me
is not what schoolbook text would be.
For I, a man whose simple life
and coloured morals born of strife
would simply not live up to those
of dear old England's "sicko" poets...

...But all's not lost, an afterthought,
for great men gone and yet unborn.
To pay respect to Langston's poetry,
whose word went up in history.

DuBois - a man able means.
A graduate in slavery.
"The Souls of Black Folk" classic work -
an unsung hero in schoolbook terms.

And those alive, who seek today
to bring the world to harmony.
Like Gil Scott Heron or *LKJ,
Jalal Nurridin - poets great.

English schools in the '70's still had their heads in colo-
nialism and had no qualms about plays like "Black Sambo in the
Jungle" or books like Enid 'Blight-on's' "10 Little Nigger Boys",
which they regarded as classics. I can remember being subject-
ed to these humiliations with horror.

It was only after meeting Gil Scott Heron that I was
exposed to Black History and discovered that we weren't gollie
wogs like on the jam jar or sambos in the jungle as I'd been led
to believe, but were as much if not more inventive and creative
than our white counterparts.

A WEB DuBois novel "The Souls of Black Folk" was a
classic 19th Century literary masterpiece. It is of note that Langston Hughs's poetry surpasses much of the curriculum material
that we read in schools today. Additionally, Gil Scott Heron's
work is one of the few accurate accounts of black people and
US politics in the '70's on record and The Last Poets depicted
life as it was and predicted how it will be for black Americans,
Muslims and non-Muslims alike.

Why can't we have some of these work's on the curriculum?

---

*Linton Kwesi Johnson (LKJ) articulated urban life from a West Indian point
of view and made no compromise in his right to deliver his poetry in his own
patois dialect. To these poets - I can relate.

Freedom is a Funny Thing!

2.
Freedom is a funny thing!
We all believe that it can be.
But dreams of youths in poverty,
when shattered by reality,
make me question our democracy,
I ask, "Are we truly free?"
If so, then freedom is a funny thing.

Freedom is a funny thing! "Ha Ha!" You think.
"Not so!" I say,
"To freedom we must find a way."
"You're free!" They say,
"Why can't you see,
long gone are chains of slavery?
This is a free democracy!
We're both as equals you and me."

"If so" I say, "We're neither free."

You talk about democracy
and equal rights for blacks and whites.
But in your eyes I see the truth,
your drunken mouth provides the proof.

There's chips on shoulders - I agree,
but fry your own before you fry me.
'cause I'm aware of your contempt
for everyone except yourself,
I'm just another category
not welcome in your bigotry,
for all your views and flattery,
I clearly see your hate for me.

If the skin you wear, was black, not fair;
you'd suffer inequality.
You'd hate so-called "democracy".
You'd writhe in pains of poverty.
If bigots said, "Why can't you see?"
And told you that, "You're truly free!"
You'd stare them right between the eyes
and from your soul I'd hear the cries;

"God help this damn democracy!"
Why can't there be equality?
Won't anyone just listen to me?
Lord! When can we be truly free?"

When from your race, you've been outcast.
You're scared and hungry and on your ass.
A song of freedom I would sing.
Now isn't freedom a funny thing?

I am continually amazed at the ignorance of the average British person, who whilst being among the most educated people in the world, have such superficial and unchallenging views on matters of culture, race, religion and politics. Whites know little or nothing about blacks. Christians know less about Muslims and politicians know even less still about the needs of those whom they profess to serve. How can it be?

This poem challenges the notion of democracy, which professes wonderful facets but to a black man in a white society, Muslims in a Christian society, or indeed a poor person in a rich society, possesses little of what it professes and in actuality is often the very opposite.

Democracy comes from two Latin terms:
1. Demos: people, and 2. Kratia: to rule. The illusion of Democracy is "rule by the people". Its literal meaning and actual application is "to rule the people".

Elena.

A tribute to Elena Dragomer of Constanta Romania.

3.
Suspended in time 1949.
Behind the iron curtain.
The 1980's she could not see,
still she listened to a song of liberty.

When I asked her out with me
our hearts and minds were one.
She played a Stevie Wonder song
and I was thinking while she sang along.

Oh why must you remain here - Elena?
To be free is your fantasy.
Free just like a river, in springtime,
flowing down to the sea,
is all you want to be.

But still she must remain here.
Romania!
Her heart's in the west - her mind the east.
Thinking of a river.
I leave her.
Wishing that she were free.
Through a blind man she can see.

Her golden hair, her skin so fair,
I'm locked in ecstasy.
Her fingers sing a song for me,
as they dance across her piano keys.

And when it's time to say good-night.
In the shadows I must run.
The very next day our dream is gone,
when we're seen together
and the police come.

Oh! Why must you remain here - Elena?
Freedom's just a word within a song.
Freedom like a river, I give her,
all of my heart this day.
For her freedom I pray.

But still she must remain here, Romania.
Suspended in time and poverty.
Thinking of a river,
I leave her.
Wishing that we were as free.
Through a blind man we can see.
Only rivers in our worlds run free.

Two weeks after writing this poem, the hated dictator Nicoli Ceaucescu was deposed by a popular uprising of the people of Romania. They tried him and sentenced both him and his wife to death. There were so many volunteers to be in the firing squad, that they had to hold a national lottery to decide who would execute him. The headquarters of his notorious secret Police, the "Securitaté" was ransacked. He was so hated, that the people televised his execution on national TV.

I was surprised when Elena played me Stevie Wonder (because his music had reached behind the iron curtain) and more so when she and her sisters were arrested by the Securitaté for being seen with a Westerner - me - and their mother had to sell the family's antique piano to pay the bribe to release them from jail.

Elena said, "I want to be free. Free like a river. Like Stevie Wonder said". I hope that one day Elena and her people can be free like a river.

Power.
A letter to those in power.

4.
Dear Power,

Can you tell me who's responsible for the economic blight that plagues my home town? You see, I've spent half a life asking why the street's run down. Where children play corruption reigns and broken dreams are wall to wall in council house and racist school.

Mother of youth naive and true, she stands faceless in unemployment queue. She's low on pharmaceutical dope. 'cause you stole her kids. 'said you'd help her cope.

You had all the answers when she signed your sheet, you'd just borrow the children 'till she was back on her feet. But when she came to take them back, "Oh we're terribly sorry - you can't do that".

The children asked, "What have we done?" The system said: "We're overrun." The social worker's on commission, "You're on the books kid. There's no remission."

The children striving to be free. The system lying, dreams are dying, mothers crying, the system's thriving.

"Cast your vote," politicians say. To ghetto youth they're all the same. He asks, "What have they done for me? It's still the same and I'm 23. I try to work, who'll take me on, if I'm from the ghetto and my skin is brown?" So I move away to where it's at. Where they take your soul, if that's all you've got.

'see there's always a market for a tender soul, from a broken home, with a dream that's bold, where they make you up - like a living doll. Then break you down when you discover what's wrong. Then groom your mane and comfort your pain, with false emotion exploit your devotion.

When they've burned you out, your heart's ragged and torn and you're cursing yourself and the day you were born. They just throw you back to the gutters of strife. At the end of the day "Hey! It's only your life."

Now you're back on the street, but who wants you around? "You traded your soul," they say, "pound for pound. You're not the same guy you used to be. You're no longer welcome as you can see. So pack your things, why don't you go? Don't call on people you used to know."

So you're back at the start potential fodder for jail. The system's laughing if they make on your bail. 'cause it don't really matter if you win or you lose. The solicitor earns and the barrister too.

Then the judge will decide just how long you'll be used. 'cause the wardens make money, the judge does too.

And society's protected from the threat that you pose and the system thrives as their industry grows. In a guise of free enterprise and justice indeed? 'see I'm no longer deceived, 'cause I know you're power and I want a reprieve.

This poem was written three years before I became a Muslim and was directed at those faceless individuals in government and their untouchable tentacles in the judiciary, who saw fit to remove an innocent 9 year old from his mother and place him behind bars with criminals. I addressed the letter to "power" to demonstrate the impersonal nature of the state entity that appears to interfere with and control our destiny.

However, since becoming a Muslim, I now know that "There is no might or power except Allah" and to him we will all answer, (including those who think that they themselves represent power). That day will be the ultimate day of reckoning.

Black & Blue.

5.
Life can be so sad,
when you're black & blue.

Running 'round in circles,
you don't know what to do.

With all the worries in the world,
beating down on you.

It's little wonder why you cry,
when you're black & blue.

Every day's a bad-old-day,
when you're black & blue.

The good times only memories
or dreams that might come true.

Night & day you ponder
what the world is coming to.

But still you're left to wonder - why -
when black, you're always blue?

It doesn't seem to matter,
what you say or do.

Close your ears and close your eyes
but still it gets to you.

To stand and fight. To run and hide.
To turn and face the truth.

That sweetness flowed from lions bones
but first came black & blue.

No one says you have to cry,
because you're black & blue.

So wipe the teardrops from your eye
and view the world anew.

Turn your worries into rhythm,
troubles into song.

'cause black and blue are as beautiful
as night and day are long.

Let it be, just what it is
and keep your mind in tact.

Like summer sun and autumn rain,
it's just a natural fact.

As long as you can bring about
the melody in you.

You'll soon find out, there's more to being black
than feeling blue.

The words "black" and "blue" have always had negative conotations for me. Primarily because the term is used to describe being bruised or damaged. I find that there are similar connotations to people's perception of being black, including my own.

This poem was an attempt to display the positive aspects of what my blackness means to me, rather than the negative perceptions that had been inculcated in me since childhood, whilst growing up in a generally hostile white society. Similar feelings in black Americans led to the development of "The Blues". By taking the hatred of the oppressor and turning it into song, the bruised victim capitalises upon the pain inflicted by his oppressor, thus turning the tables on him.

Black & Tan.
I want my culture back.

6.
What would you say,
if I told you what I am?
A human man - of black and tan.
Black as my heritage. African line.
Tan as my skin colour, starved of sunshine.

Starved in a world where the sun rarely shines.
Robbed is my heritage. Tanned is my hide.

Tanned is my hide every time I rise up.
And question the thieves that my heritage took.
Starved of a future. A world without war.
Starved of a chance to make good - by the law.

What would you call me if I said to you
That "You are responsible for all that I do?"
If I did a murder or drugs or made war.
Would you give me medals my country adore?
Would you give me power to kill and to steal?
Would you let me make law to guard such ideals?

I think not somehow, though ironic it is;
that you do for you all these things and do with:

A power you stole from my African line.
Abused and misused like my people through time.
By you and your laws made for keeping us down.
& tanning my hide 'cause my skin colour's brown.
I want you to know "tan enough is my skin and
one day we'll return - back our culture, we'll win".

Much of contemporary western knowledge was derived
from the African Muslims during their 600 year rule of Spain,
Portugal, Southern France, Sicily, Malta and the Balearics. It
was acquired during the "re-conquista" in 1482 and made Spain
and Portugal super powers. The power was used for African
Slavery and American genocide.

Innervision.
A tribute to Stevie Wonder.

7.
In this world, in which we live
the qualities of life we have to give,
would seem no more to men with sight
than formless shadows in the night.

The men of power - proud and loud.
Their voices echoing through the crowds
of men and women blind with fear
of all they see and all they hear.

And what becomes of those with vision
of all men equal - with no division?
They're quickly killed or thrown in prison,
to dream alone of truth and freedom.

While those with eyes, see only lies.
And those with ears hear only sneers.
There's something else that baffles me
If the truth is the light,
how come the blind still see?

Inner visions are out of sight,
like distant stars in broad daylight.
Except to those who have not eyes
and in whose hearts true vision lies.

Blindness of the eyes is a physical condition which limits
the blind person from viewing their surroundings in a normal
way. However the eyes aren't the only human facet that sees.
The heart has its own capacity for sight, though not in the physical sense but rather the metaphysical or spiritual sense. It is
clear that people with normal vision often cannot see. The prob-
lem is, that whilst their eyes behold something, the blindness of
their hearts forbids them from comprehending it. A blind man,
who cannot be deluded by a visual facade, may have vision in
his heart, which allows him to see what a seeing person with a
blind heart cannot.

Destiny.
(Not for sale!)

8.
Everybody has a reason to live.
Everyone has got something to give.
Whatever it is,
it's got to be true.
To find your destiny
is something you've got to do.

'cause the world just moves through stages
in time and space (can't set the pace.)
The problems are part of the make-up of life
There's troubles and strife
You've got to fight for your rights.

People talkin' 'bout, "You're working for me.
As long as I pay,
you do what I say."
They say, "Fame & fortune may be yours for the take,"
but their only concern,
is the money they'll make.

Taking lives and bartering souls.
Chasin' rainbows that you never can hold.
Making rules just to suit their own need.
With never a thought about the dirt in the deed.

But who needs a rainbow,
any place but the sky?
Who needs to suffer
and who wants to die?
Who makes the money
and who knows why?
When all the best things in life
money can't buy?

Bourbon St.
(New Orleans.)

9.
If you've ever wondered, where to wander
when Mississippi don't seem fair.
Take a taxi cab, to Bourbon Street
and the blues - you'll find it there.

Oh there's the shoeshine man.
With black and tan.
And the children tap their heels.
For a quarter, a dime
or a dollar-a-time,
entertainment on the street.

Walk through "The Famous Door".
Where Dixiland - played since 1934,
There's a sister swingin' at "Papa Joes"
Don't you know that's the French quarter?.

I heard them singin' the blues,
in a cocktail bar,
where the tourists sing along.
And the brother on the microphone apologised,
when they asked for the national anthem.

But I don't mind. 'cause I saw them dollars flow,
into the bottle on the piano
and the pianist smiled at me.
And for a dollar and a dime, he played "Misty" for me.
The sweetest memory, I have of New Orleans.

Our ship docked in Baton Rouge, Louisiana on the Mississippi delta and I wanted to go ashore. I was told that I couldn't
go ashore in Baton Rouge with any white sailor, as blacks and
whites could not mix freely. This is 1989 America. Home of
democracy! I was disgusted and decided to go further afield into
neighbouring New Orleans, which was said to be a little more
cosmopolitan. This poem is a snapshot of what I found there.

Mark on tour
with Gil Scott Heron (1987).

Malik's Hajj to Mecca with Jalal of "The Last Poets" (2002).

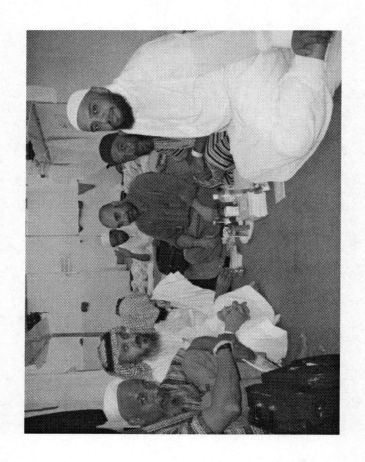

Mark, Robbie Gordon & Rod Youngs (G.S.H Band) at Blues Alley (1988).

Reg' (Slow Train) Watson & Prime Minister Burnham of Guyana 1966.

Richie Havens live on stage Sommerville MA. USA (1988).

Malik reading for an
MSc. at University (2002).

Malik in Mecca (2003).

Jalal in Mecca (2002).

The Ship's Cook.

10.
You piss me off most every day.
In your own sly-silly way.
You act like a child without a playmate.
You're about as exciting as a dirty steak-plate.
You pace the galley, all day long
and cringe each time I sing a song.
Which makes me sing a whole lot more.
If cringe you will, right out the door.

'cause when you had your boys aboard,
you schemed and lied and set up fraud.
And sent me off to Coventry
because your thief, I would not be.
But now your boys have all gone home
and left you scheming all alone.
And I've returned from Coventry,
except with you, which shows to me.

That you were at the heart of that,
which turned a good trip into bad
and paved the way for more to come.
I hope one day you'll overcome:

The rat that lives within your soul.
The hatred in your heart so cold.
The loneliness that you must feel
resulting from your dirty deal.

As a steward on a Danish oil tanker, I was subservient to the ship's cook. This particular guy from Newcastle gave me an envelope containing several hundred Dollars and said "It's a gift from the laundry man". It turns out that he was scamming the shipping company, by putting in false invoices for laundry that didn't exist and getting a kickback from the laundry firm. I refused to accept the bribe and returned it. He said, "You shouldn't have done that," and set me up, to get me sacked by accusing me of stealing. He failed, but made my voyage a misery.

The Summer Night Syndrome.
Princess Park, Liverpool, UK.

11.
Vibrant sensations flow through me,
as the soft warm night air
gently caresses my brow.

The moon casts bold shadows,
whilst its radiance sends silent echoes down my spine.

A shimmering reflection slides peacefully
from shore to shore.
Occasionally unzipped by the passing of a duck
with her eager offspring.

The distant hooting of the tawny owl
enhances the somewhat tense feeling
of the summer night syndrome,
whilst the warmth and peace of the evening air,
gently reassures the senses,
of safe conduct through the moonlit night.

I pause to observe the anticipating eyes
that pierce the night skies.
Ferociously luminous,
set in poised feline features.

A dry twig crunches beneath my feet.
I glance down at the earth and quickly look up
and the eyes are no more.

I relax, then continue home.
Once again having fallen prey
to the seduction of
"the summer night syndrome".

Mediterranean Sunset.

Off the coast of Libya.

12.

The last hour of day rests wearily.
Its silent radiance dancing across the smooth blue.
The redness of its power,
cutting through the grey-cloud mountain top,
spilling down its slopes in volcanic-like beauty.

The haze on the horizon fades as I look up.
Blending softly into a deep blue backdrop,
where a lone white wisp of nature
hangs sullen in the darkening skies,
frowning at the scene below.

Behind us lie the Gibraltar straits.
The passage by which mother Atlantic
gave birth to this aquatic wonderland.
Ahead, the mysteries of its Aegean offspring
guardian of the Dardanelles
and birthplace to many a Greek legend.

I can feel you now.
Your beauty touches me within.
The sweet scent of African shores
ignites my sixth sense.

I yearn to touch her as you do.
Though as I reach out toward her,
only my spirit can caress her wandering coastline.
And as the shadows of night draw near,
so falls the veil that separates our hearts.

A grey fleet of stars and stripes patrol the still waters.
An intimidating deterrent.
An armoured peace corps,
ready to strike Tripoli at a moments notice.

A chill runs through my veins
as the war 'copter scrutinizes our home.
My blood turns cold with every motion of its
killing blades as they cut through my peace.

The lone white wisp of nature no longer frowns,
for its work is done and the last hour of day is gone.
To the moon and stars alone does the evening belong.

This night as we sleep both you and I,
let the light of the moon shine down a truce
between ships of war and African shore.

Show the people of the world the natural
beauty of the elements they seek to destroy.
Let the unselfishness of the passage of day
into night be an example to us all.
Instill in our hearts, the secret of your calm,
so we both might know peace until dawn?

This poem was written from the deck of an oil tanker off the
coast of Libya. Ronald 'Ray-Gun' was the US president at the
time and George Bush Sr. was his vice president. It was around
this time that the USA decided to bomb Libya and had its 7th
fleet in the Mediterranean for precisely that reason.

The Americans flew helicopter gun ships over all shipping
in that area and anyone whom they suspected of trading with
Libya, was simply blown out of the water if they refused to obey
the USA. This is an example of democracy at its finest.

Mist of the East.
Across the North Atlantic to Finnistare.

13.
The sun creeps out from behind the mist.
Solar beams dash across the waves in all directions.
A hint of blue skies appear, amid the harshness
of the deep grey clouds.

An uncanny atmosphere surrounds the vessel.
A strange humidity appears to rise, as the mist
begins to crawl away from the sun in the east,
slowly, sneakily, bringing with it all manner of mystery.

The ship rolls as the mist climbs aboard.
Unfurling itself like a dense cloud along the main deck,
over the bridge, across the poop and sealing us aft'
like salami in wax paper, sweltering in the
unnaturalness of our assumed protective skin.
Awaiting its silent departure.

Mist of the morning won't you leave us be?
Peel back your moistened skin.
Return to the grey skies from whence you came
and take with you that westerly wind.
That merciless draught you've cast on our beam.
Stealin' our sleep and our peace and our dreams.
Rendering us helpless in the path of your stream.

Allow us a passage across the great sea.
We head for the shores of our Spanish retreat.
We mean you no harm, all we want is your calm.
Let us travel in peace - through you - mist of the east.

Nature.

14.
Nature is so gracefully cruel,
it can but be admired.
Its power far surpasses that of men and their desires.
For nature has the final say,
when all seems said and done.
And still presides despite attempts by man to overcome it.

Now nature's always tried so hard,
to share with everyone,
its wonders and phenomena from which we all can learn.
But ignorant and dis-concerned we suddenly become.
When money overrides our cares
and governs all but one.

'cause what would all the cash be worth
if nature wasn't there?
No mountain tops, no rain, no sun
or freshness in the air.
No flowers, trees or animals
to share the planet's face.
No human form, no dusk or dawn
only darkness in its place.

'see nature is no simple fool
to toy with and abuse.
Pollute, plough down,
cement and drown,
destroying all that's used.
Even nature in its patience
can but take so much.
Before retaliation strikes
and someone bites its dust.

Slow Train.

A tribute to my father: Born 30/03/1918.

15.

Slow Train! He was a Slow Train!
An' now that Slow Train, keeps on movin' in my mind.
Slow Train! Beating down a one way track.
He was a Slow Train! I know he's never coming back.
An' now that Slow Train, keeps on movin' in my mind.
Slow Train! Out there in the sun and rain.
Slow Train! Cuttin' through that sugar cane.
They say that Slow Train was doing fine.

Just short of his manhood, he was young and free.
Met a fine woman, start to spread his seed.
Too hot to handle. Too young to know.
He'd be fighting for his life when her man came home.
Signed on a tramp ship in Bartica Bay.
Sailed around the globe 'till up his number came.
Wartime waterfront a living hell,
but he lived long enough to let his children tell;

about the Slow Train! Beating down a one way track.
He was a Slow Train! I know he's never coming back.
An' now that Slow Train, keeps on movin' in my mind.
Slow Train! Out there in the sun and rain.
Slow Train! Dreamin' 'bout that sugar cane.
He was a Slow Train, but right on time.

Twilight blues, they set in bye and bye
but he never made a stop 'till his steam ran dry.
Working overtime 'till his engines died.
Now he's riding on that great track in the sky.

He was a Slow Train! Beating down a one way track.
Slow Train! I know he's never coming back.
He's just a Slow Train, keeps on riding through the skies.
Slow Train! Out there in the sun and rain.
Slow Train! Cuttin' through that sugar cane.
I know that Slow Train left me his lines.

If Only?

16.

If only I'd been born a day later than I was.
I'd have been a battle ram, like the father that I lost.
Alas! I am the fish, in troubled waters do I swim.
In never ending circles, in pursuit of my tail fin.
If only I had listened to myself more as a child.
Done only what I thought was right,
my conscience as my guide.
My school I'd never skip. From children's home I'd never run.
But now it's far too late you see the damage has been done.

If only I'd had faith in my ability in PE.
I'd be Olympic swimmer now, not sailor lost at sea.
Or maybe swim the Channel, as the teacher once did hope.
But now I smoke so much that I can barely swim a stroke.

If only comprehensive school, I'd taken seriously.
I'd surely be in college, bound for university.
Now all I do is wash the pots when workers finish tea.
I clean up all the shit they leave. Their legacy to me.

If only I had been less quick to speak my mind at work.
A chef I'd be in French cuisine, in Paris or Dunkirk.
But now the only prospect of promotion in that line.
Is slaving over galley stoves for racists all my life.

If only I had learnt from people I'd seen trapped in debt.
My money I'd have never blown, while trying to impress.
The moral fibre of my life would still be quite in tact.
With people who had cared for me, I'd still be back-to-back.

If only I could sing the Blues, 'bout chances I have blown.
Or play the saddest melody, if I could blow the saxophone.
I'd never take for granted gifts the Lord did give to me.
If I felt good inside, I'd be content with poverty.
But life's too short to cry about the things I haven't done.
For what I do now, paves the way for things I've yet to come.
I'll try to do my best, with good potential others see.
But still retain my self respect, while simply being me.

See the Light.

17.
As I look out from the balcony,
a chapter closes in front of me.
I see a lifetime and a history.
I know the future's not ours to see.

(Chorus)
Every sunrise brings a new day,
every new day in our life,
brings the dewdrops in the morning
and the moonlight in the night.
There's a place for everyone
who's lost and searchin' for a light.
But you've got to start believing,
if you want to see the light.

As I lie awake this lonely night,
hoping and praying for some company.
I stop just for a little while,
to hear the voice that's callin' out to me.

(Chorus)
Every sunrise brings a new day,
every new day in our life,
brings the dewdrops in the morning
and the moonlight in the night.
There's a place for everyone
who's lost and searchin' for a light.
But you've got to start believing,
if you want to see the light.

When I wrote this song, I was influenced by reading reli-
gious texts, although it would be some 6 years before that light
would manifest itself, in the form of the faith of Islam within my
soul. This song is indicative of my quest for knowledge whilst
travelling the world and upon reflection, one can see clearly
where such a quest would lead. All thanks and praise are due to
Allah.

Africa.

18.
Africa! With your misty morning.
Hear my heart! It's beggin' I'm calling.
Africa! Won't you shine a light for me?

Though I travel as an English man.
I've been searchin' for my fatherland.
At last I'm so close I can see,
my Africa in front of me.

Oh, Africa! With your misty morning.
Hear my heart! It's beggin' I'm calling.
Africa! Won't you shine a light for me?

Deprivation is in our land.
But starvation I just don't understand.
When there's enough food for everyone.
All we have to do is spread it around.

In Africa! With your misty morning.
Hear my heart! It's beggin' I'm calling.
Africa! Won't you shine a light for me?

I know you're a troubled place.
You're carrying the burdens of every race.
I hope that one day you'll be free,
so I can go home through my family tree;

To my Africa! With your misty morning.
Hear my heart! It's beggin' I'm calling.
Africa! Won't you shine a light for me?
Oh Africa!

This poem was written on the deck of the ship which first
took me to Africa but unable to go ashore, I could only dream
about the homeland that my forefathers were stolen from.

Blues.

A sailor's reflections of life in London, whilst at sea.

19.

When your life is such a mess.
You're so confused.
You've been looking for a place,
where you can buy some booze,
or something like that.

When you think you've got it made.
And you realise.
that it's falling apart,
and you just wanna get high,
let the blues go by.

(Chorus.)
Don't walk away from your troubles.
There's still a chance.
You've got to stand up strong.
Just got to climb that wall.
Then you can carry on.
You'll only reach the other side,
if you really want to.
Doesn't matter where you run,
or any place you try to hide.
You've still got to carry on.

Have you ever been sailing
on the timeless seas,
when the memory of the people,
that you love and need
make you wanna go home?

Ever thought you had it right,
tinsel town and flashing lights?
Discovering that you were wrong,
don't wanna face the facts
you've still got to carry on. *(Repeat chorus.)*

Winds of Change.

20.
Riding on the tides of a midnight moon.
Summer heat in the darkness, an' a breeze blowin' through.
My mind's telling me, things will be alright.
As a new day dawns I can feel its might.

It's only the winds of change, breezin' through the darkness.
Only the winds of change can make things right.

So don't you worry none my brother,
generations to come will know your name.
Don't you worry none my sister,
you're the mother of tomorrow's freedom brains.
Because times will change
and people will come to know themselves
and the truth will be - eternal - one and all will see,
that the light of truth shines endlessly.

It's only the winds of change that will make what's been so
wrong, turn towards what's right.
Only the winds of change breezin' through the night.

Don't you ever get to sit and ponder on life,
while you're looking at the stars in the dead of the night?
Somehow the heavens reach out to you, with the solutions
to the problems you've been wadin' through.
While the moon caresses your troubled brow.
And the heat of the darkness makes you feel somehow;
though your body is sweating, there's a breeze comin'
through, that will cool the pain that's left you feeling blue.

And only the winds of change. Only the winds of change.
Only the winds of change, can put things right.
Only the winds of change. Only the winds of change.
It's only the winds of change, breezin' through the night.

Get Up!

21.
Get up!
Shake loose the self-enslaving shackles of regret.

Rise up!
And be sublime, your life is yours to love and live.

Wake up!
Take in the sunlight as the morning brings to you.
A chance to make a difference, in the light of all things new.

Get up!
Just try again. Don't lay there helpless on the ground.

Dry up!
Those tears, let happy spirits fill the world around.

Wake up!
Savour the sweetness of a summers morning dew
and all that mother nature in her wonder bears for you.

The jewel of life,
an entity so precious in itself.

The seeds of love.
For you to sow a natural source of wealth.

A world in which to live,
with all the tools to make it through.

The gift of sight for you to see just what you have to do...
Get up!

Someone once told me, *"It's better to be a 'has been' - than a 'could have been'."* That statement often helped me to "get up" when I felt like giving up.

Cherish the Good Man.

Inspired by 'Tünç' a student in Izmit Turkey.

22.

Cherish the good man, for they are rare upon the earth.
Cherish the wise man. Then from his wisdom you will learn.
You've got to listen to the prophecies.
The old and the young still have something to learn.
Why don't you listen to the prophecies?
You'll never be sorry for what you have heard.

(Chorus)
'cause it's a cruel earth, we live upon.
Everyone is familiar with the situation.
If you're true and strong, you can't go wrong.
If you cherish the good man.

Cherish the woman. The bringer of life.
Cherish the mothers of the world,
don't make them suffer all their lives.
You've got to cherish every land and sea.
Pollution and destruction does not hold the key.
You've got to cherish every land and sea.
So future generations will have something to eat.

'cause it's a cruel earth, we live upon.
Everyone is familiar with the situation.
If you're true and strong, you can't go wrong.
If you cherish the good man.

Got to learn from the wise man.
Got to protect the womb-man (woman).
You've got to listen to the prophet man.
Got to stop this pollution.
And this mindless destruction.
Got to respect the land and sea.
Got to set all the mothers free, from economic captivity.
And your wars and political greed.
Your rockets and your senseless needs.
Nuclear testing and mindless deeds. *(ad lib).*

Fruit of My Love.

A reflection of a young girl's pain after having an abortion.

23.

A Fore-Word to the poem:

I examine the figure of dark silken skin and remember how I longed to hold that hand. The swell in her womb, unwelcome like a rugged grey mountain in the midst of green fields, prolongs my gaze.

As I listen to the story of the grey mountain, I can feel her pain. With every word like a wrench on my heart, as the tale of unborn life unfolds and the rare gift of inner sight, allows me to endure every painstaking second of her sad recollection.

I glance at the 'surrounding influence' to this dark starlet and see with my mind's eye, a sickening mixture of bad advice and submissive agreement. I reach out to touch her sadness, to make it my own but I become conscious of the surrounding influence and retreat into the dark leather chair, that somehow offers sanctuary from my discomfort.

I look into her eyes, then at those who surround her so obligingly and I see a tree. A solid dark oak, strong as the years but with the quaint beauty of a sapling. The influences that surround her in her unbalanced state of grief, appear to me to be her only branches.

I think again of the tree she represents and it occurs to me that it's sometimes better to remove the branches in order to save the tree. But alas, I am not the wood cutter, just a nature lover.

The following is probably the hardest poem I've ever had to write. Not least because of the traumatic subject matter and the helpless inability to reverse the process, but because as a man, it is impossible to feel what a woman feels in such a situation. Trying to reach inside someone else's soul and amply articulate 'their' pain is indeed difficult.

Fruit of My Love.

The poem.

24.

The time has come.
The choice is mine to make and mine alone.
The one I love, I cannot find,
can't take it any more.
When everything seemed set and sure,
I just can't face alone...
Fruit of my love, oh! Just what have I done?

Sometimes love I dream of us, together in my world.
Playing, laughing in the park,
then dancing home again.
Morning comes and I awake,
to find myself alone.
Fruit of my love, oh! Where have you gone?

Life must go on. I know.
Every time I think of you, the hurt begins to grow.
I hope that you will understand,
wherever your spirit roams,
you're more than just a memory,
you're part of me... For evermore.

And evermore.
Fruit of my love, wherever you are?
You're by my side, my conscious guide
My love won't die, for you I cry.
You'll be with me, eternally.
You're in my heart, wherever I'll be.

You're by my side, my guiding light,
I cry each night, my fear I fight.
You'll be with me, eternally.
The fruit of my love
You'll always be.
You'll always be.
You'll always be...

The Lonely Dreamer.
Reflections on touring with Gil Scott Heron & Richie Havens.

A Fore-Word to the poem:
25.

February has been designated as 'black history month' in America and in 1988, I toured the east coast with Gil Scott Heron on a black history month tour, combined with the legendary sixties black folk music master, Richie Havens. Richie was the opening act on that very first "Woodstock" concert in the USA.

I first met Richie that year, at a gig in the 'Inter-Media Art Centre' in Huntington, NY. He was chillin' backstage in a cool African dashiki and had a kufi hat on. I didn't know who he was until Gil introduced us but I remember thinking that - "this brother looks cool".

Richie was a man of few words and Gil and Richie had a kind of way of communicating without speaking much, they just seemed to know what each other meant. I remember standing there between them in silence. It was like being sandwiched between two giants, not because of their stature, (we were all about the same height) but the charisma of these musical pioneers, made a brother like me feel humbled in their presence.

After what felt like an eternity, Gil broke the silence. "Hey Richie!" Gil exclaimed. "What it is?" Replied Richie. "This here is brother Mark from England. 'Met this brother on the road. Brother-man was lookin' for the truth." "Way it should be man," replied Richie. "Way it should be." That was my endorsement, Richie and me were cool thereafter.

Gil loved his band to solo during the performance and when pianist Kim Jordan solo'd, it was like a rolling river. Kim also read the scriptures a lot, so I use the analogy *"roll river Jordan"* for her. Bass guitarist - Robbie Gordon, was designated by Gil as the *"secretary of entertainment"* responsible for maintaining *"the vibeosphere"*. Robbie later became known as Abdul Hadi.

Footnotes to the poem on the next page:
*'Spider'. (A nickname for Gil Scott Heron.)
**'Hollow-way'. (Play on words) Ron Holloway - Gil's saxophonist.
***'The master of disaster'. (A nickname for drummer Rod Youngs.)

The Lonely Dreamer.
The poem.

26.

Thoughts of home and the feeling's strong,
about all I've been missing and where I went wrong.
I'm just another lonely dreamer on the seven seas.
I've declined a dinner with royalty.
I've shunned invitations to the embassy,
to be with a travelling blues band,
people who still care and can understand...
The highs and lows of real life.
The twilight days and urban nights.
The brothers at the bottom of a bottle of wine.
The yesterday's heroes and the day before's crimes.

'Spiders' smile we all understand,
means roll *'river Jordan'* to the promised land.
And the **'hollow-way'* of the saxophone,
sends the melodies echoing through my soul.
Though the ***'master of disaster',* is out of sight.
The rhythm of the drum beats through the night.
The *'entertainment secretary'*, on the bass
is my main man Robbie G.

But I know I'll be blue before I'll be free,
to be again with the folks I want to be.
And the blues ain't nothing but a good man feeling bad.
Though my travelling days are sad and long,
that's the price that I'm paying, for where I went wrong.
I can hear Richie Havens telling me,
"What it is brother-man, just let it be."

But from the blues I've learnt one vital thing.
You've got to hold on to all your dreams.
My daddy's dream, he used to say,
was to take me back home to the sugar cane.
My childhood dream was to sail the seas,
like my daddy did before he had me.
But I never thought that I would be,
Just another lonely dreamer on the seven seas.

Cartogena.
(Pronounced 'Cartaheyna').

27.

Cartogena; you sit upon a Colombian coastal corner, sneering at the sea. Jeering at the jungle of a once beautiful land where now you are in familiar Manhattan style.

Stand proud oh Cartogena and show the visiting world how fat you are. How well you've tamed the native. How grateful "your-Afro-His-panic" should be, that you allow him to paddle his dug-out canoe across your bay. To trade his baby crocodiles to ships that pass through in the night. How clichéd Cartogena?

How rich oh Cartogena? How rich you are. Is it really yours? Or does your wealth belong to another? The jungle perhaps? Or maybe "your-Afro-His-panic" and his dug-out canoe?

How bold Cartogena? How boldly you batter the natives' jungle backwards. Away from your thriving coastline and into the blackness of the distant night. Swaying cutlass and snake-bitten ankle. Bulldozing mercilessly. Loyal to your sovereignty. Once a week, perhaps, feeding the family.

Something stinks Cartogena and it's not the jungle. Something stinks far worse than the dead baby crocodiles in the dug-out canoe. Let's take a look Cartogena? Let's take a long hard look at what you've done? Why not start with the man? The black man. (Seen as we already know about the jungle.)

His skin clutches the bone beneath, while yours ripples over the snakeskin belt that surrounds your waist. His hands bear the scars of poverty and toil, whilst yours bear the golden rings of his toil. His feet are as rotten as the dead croc's in his dug-out, whilst your tender paws are clad in crocodile skin shoes, that you watched him suffer to make. How clever Cartogena?

Wasn't it cool the way you swerved your $10,000 water bike about the stern of the visiting world? How impressed we were. Oh Cartogena, you're so fair!

A Hood Rat's Respect.
Who needs it?

28.
What should I do, to get hood rats respect?
You say I can't get it unless I act vexed.
I've respect of my own, an' I'm human - like you.
Only those I respect, will I give it to.

But my respect I hold in check, until I'm sure of your intent.
I realise people are prone to change.
But for my respect, I hold the reins.
First I look to see what you and your respect want me to do.
You act like I should seek your favour.
And show you that I've got some flavour.

So consequently I wrote these lines,
to set the record straight one-time.
To gain respect on ghetto street,
I first must have the cash to meet;
the standards set by ghetto kings
and drive the car and do the things,
that make the money for the image -
renounce my soul and purge my heritage.
Sell my sister, beat my brother.
Kill my gran' and rob my mother.
Turn the children from their innocence.
Guide them to a life of decadence.
Junkies, whores and drunken fathers,
were brothers, sisters and parental guardians.
Dropouts, winos, pros and cons.
Robbers, rapists all in one - big consequence of urban life.
Resulting from a common strife.

Respect I have, does not come cheap,
like cars and cash and ghetto streets.
Though your respect, I may not boast.
My self respect I value most.
Above your gold and diamond rings.
Your flashy cars and ghetto kings.

The Sea.

29.
All is still at midnight, in no-man's-land.
All except our home, that is.
Bow like razor's edge, cutting seas in two.
A mobile equator, distinguishing the tropics
of port and starboard.
Each reminiscent of our passage,
only by the stretch of motorway
that trails back from our after end, towards the horizon,
highlighted by the silvery gaze of the full moon.

A wisp of dark smoke
slithers silently from the funnel.
As if stretching out towards the distant stars.
But reaching only the moon,
before disappearing into the cotton-candy cloud,
that caresses the moon's face
as it glides slowly by.

All is silent at midnight.
All except the constant chuddering of the propeller,
that churns out our trail.
Our legacy to the sea.

You harmonise with the elements at sea,
for they often affect your fate.
The sun provides our daylight.
Night light and tides - by the moon.
The wind takes charge of the waves.
And nature cares for them all.

The Lord takes care of nature,
in this world of water,
that we have come to love
and call our home.

The Rainbow Haze.

30.
I look to the water's edge.
Only to see the burning sun descending slowly
like a bubble falling to earth.
Then, as if by some miracle of nature,
being cooly consumed by the liquid horizon.

The rainbow haze, a now familiar sight at sunset,
lingers to provide a fitting backdrop for the eager photographer
who arrived too late to catch the sun's daily demise.

As if almost anticipating the photographer's glare
through speedy lens,
the gannets embark upon a strategically timed fly-by.
Breaking the subtle monotony of the stillness,
that provides the invisible shroud
that's draped casually across the haze.

The moon is hiding still. But where? I know not.
I can feel her presence silently waiting, patient as life.
To make her inevitable entry onto the stage of night.

Then alas! Her evening accomplices will provide a new light.
To form an unprecedented, untouchable alternative
to what have become for me the "living days".
Privy as I am, by sheer fortune alone,
to the life giving rays of that now familiar
rainbow haze.

You might not think that there could be so many ways to
describe a sunset but what you witness at sea cannot easily be
put into words. The water surrounds you on all sides and nothing
but the horizon restricts your view at this marvel of nature. What
I came to realise when leaving the city, where very few people
look at the stars or the sunset, is that no two sunsets are ever
the same. No doubt there is a poem in every one of them.

S.O.S.

31.
Sentenced by the Lord to live a life upon the earth.
A chance to pay our dues,
our debt back to the universe.
But every way we try to move,
there's always someone there.
Try to stop us. Make us change our minds.
Are we going anywhere?

(Chorus)
Or are we captive within this earthly dome?
Like fishes inside a goldfish bowl.
Just eating the small to make us grow.
In the hope that the bigger the fish.
The bigger the bowl.

Everyone's a victim from the bottom to the top.
The big fish eat the small fish,
then the sharks just eat the lot.
Why can't everyone just be content with what they are?
There's still a chance we can "Save Our Souls"
if we put our trust in Allah.

'Cause we're living inside a goldfish bowl.
We're captive.
Don't know where to go.
We eat the small to make us grow.
In the hope that the bigger the fish.
The bigger the bowl.

'Cause we're living inside a goldfish bowl.
We're so confused, we've lost control.
The answers lie within our souls.
But all we can see are bigger bowls.

Time Eludes Me Still.

32.
Seasons flash by me.
Time eludes me.
Moments inspire me.
Systems remind me.

A constant elbow in the ear.
A regular smog in the air.
A secret enemy to fear.
A thought seed to rear.
Yet time eludes me.

A hustle here.
A shuffle there.
A changing of hands
in a constant sphere.

A vision clear.
A shedded tear.
A bustling illusion.
A mass of confusion.
And yet time eludes me.

That old devil pollution.
The great contradiction.
A righteous solution.
A moment of passion.
A pot of poison.

This place is really happening.
And yet time eludes me still.

Urbane Guerrilla.

Inspired by & dedicated to - Gil Scott Heron.

33.
Urban guerrilla learnt how to fight.
Out on the street, in the heart of the night.
Seed of a motherland far from sight,
urban guerrilla took flight.

Out in the suburbs, far from home.
He was up from an urban twilight zone.
Through pains of hunger and fears untold,
urban guerrilla kept hold.

Dropped in a jungle of vanity.
Suburban pretence and snobbery.
"Do like the monkey. Do like you see.
Forget about life on the urban scene.
You've rode the crest of suburban waves.
Learnt how to do things the urbane way".
While behind that suburban face there lay,
the scars of an urban reality.

Like the evolution of slavery.
For the revolution of industry.
In a guise of supercilious sovereignty.
The devolution of humanity.

Missing links in the chain of history,
leave the truth like a lock without a key.
Martin Luther had a freedom dream.
Malcolm X - "by any means necessary".

Mandela wouldn't compromise his freedom,
while apart-hate's killin' off his people.
Steve Biko died for what he believed in
equality for all men - justice for an urbane guerrilla.

Urbane: Cultured, debonair or refined.
Urban: Of the city.